Japanese Reader Collection Volume 2: Momotaro, the Peach Boy

Plus *Usagi to Kame*

Clay & Yumi Boutwell

www.KotobaInc.com
www.TheJapanShop.com

ISBN: 1484191137
ISBN-13: 978-1484191132

INTRODUCTION

The key to learning vocabulary is, quite simply, reading. Not only are you more likely to pick up words that interest you, but you also learn them in context. We hope this book will help with this goal.

FOR BEGINNERS

Momotaro, the Peach Boy is suitable for those new to Japanese. You will need to learn hiragana first, but we are also including furigana (small kana over kanji) and romaji so you can be sure you are reading with the correct pronunciation.

MP3s

Included, at no extra charge, are MP3s of the stories. One is read at the normal speed and the other at a slow, easy-to-follow speed. If the MP3s were not included when you purchased this book, **please see the last page for a download link.** If you have ANY trouble downloading, please email us at **help@thejapanshop.com.**

ABOUT THIS BOOK

This book contains several versions of the two stories. First, we have the story with every vocabulary word defined and explained below. Next, we go through major grammatical patterns found in the story. After that, read the story with no English and in natural Japanese (kanji with furigana included). Lastly, we are including a simple English translation, which should be avoided until you are sure you understand the story or if you find it too difficult to figure out on your own.

You may want to try to read the story in natural Japanese first. Or if you are a beginner, it may be better to go through the vocabulary before reading. Any way you do it, this book offers several ways to read, listen, and learn.

Lastly, we would love to hear from you. If you have any suggestions to make this and other books better, please let us know.

Clay & Yumi Boutwell
help@thejapanshop.com
http://www.TheJapanShop.com
http://www.TheJapanesePage.com

P.S. Please see the last page to find the download link for the MP3s of these stories free of charge.

CONTENTS

桃太郎

Story One:

Momotaro, the Peach Boy

with Running Gloss

桃太郎(ももたろう)

むかし、むかし、あるところにおじいさんとおばあさんが住(す)んでいました。 おじいさんは、山(やま)へたきぎを拾(ひろ)いに、おばあさんは、

むかし、むかし *mukashi mukashi*—a long time ago [This is the most common way to begin Japanese fairy tales.]
あるところに *aru tokoro ni*—in a certain place
おじいさん *ojiisan*—an old man; grandfather
と *to*—and
おばあさん *obaasan*—an old lady; grandmother
が *ga*—[a particle that marks the subject or something important]
住んでいました *sunde imashita*—lived
おじいさん *ojiisan*—old man; grandfather
は *wa*—[topic marker: as for the grandfather, he...]
山 *yama*—mountain
へ *e*—to; toward
たきぎ *takigi*—firewood
を *wo*—[direct object marker]
拾いに *hiroi ni*—to pick up; to gather
おばあさんは *obaasan wa*—as for the old woman, she...

川(かわ)へ洗濯(せんたく)に出(で)かけました。

おばあさんが川(かわ)で洗濯(せんたく)をしていると、川上(かわかみ)のほうから、大(おお)きな桃(もも)が「どんぶらこ、どんぶらこ」と流(なが)れてきました。

川へ *kawa e*—to the river; toward the river
洗濯に *sentaku ni*—to do washing
出かけました *dekakemashita*—left; went (to do washing)
おばあさん *obaasan*—old woman; grandmother
が *ga*—[often marks the subject]
川で *kawa de*—at the river
洗濯 *sentaku*—washing (clothes)
を *wo*—[direct object marker]
していると *shiteiru to*—upon doing...
川上 *kawakami*—upper area of a river; where the river flows from
のほうから *no hou kara*—from that direction
大きな *ookina*—a large...
桃 *momo*—peach
どんぶらこ *donburako*—plop; splash (sound)
と *to*—[particle that marks the sound the peach was making]
流れてきました *nagarete kimashita*—came washing down

おばあさんは、大喜(おおよろこ)びで、「こんなに大(おお)きな桃(もも)はみたことがない。うちに持(も)って帰(かえ)っておじいさんと一緒(いっしょ)に食(た)べましょう。」

おばあさんは、桃(もも)を家(いえ)に持(も)って帰(かえ)りました。

おばあさんは *obaasan wa*—as for the grandmother, she...
大喜び *ooyorokobi*—great joy [大 big + 喜び joy]
大喜びで *ooyorokobi de*—with great joy
こんなに *konna ni*—such as this; like this
大きな *ookina*—large; big
桃 *momo*—peach
は *wa*—[topic marker]
みたことがない *mitakoto ga nai*—haven't seen; have never seen
うちに *uchi ni*—to home; to the house
持って帰って *motte kaette*—return holding (the peach); bring home
おじいさん *ojiisan*—old man; grandfather
と一緒に *to issho ni*—together with
食べましょう *tabemashou*—let's eat
おばあさん *obaasan*—old lady; grandmother
を *wo*—[direct object marker]
家に *ie ni*—to the house
持って帰りました *motte kaerimashita*—brought (it home)

　山から帰ってきたおじいさんは、大きな桃を見てびっくりしましたが、「これは立派な桃だ。さっそく切ってみよう。」と包丁で桃を

山 *yama*—mountain
から *kara*—from (the mountain)
帰ってきた *kaettekita*—returned (from the mountain)
おじいさん *ojiisan*—the old man
は *wa*—[topic marker]
大きな *ookina*—large; big [use *na* when connecting with a noun]
桃 *momo*—peach
を *wo*—[direct object marker]
見て *mite*—saw [the て form connects 見て with びっくり "saw and was surprised."]
びっくりしました *bikkuri shimashita*—was surprised
が *ga*—but; however
これは *kore wa*—as for this, it is...
立派な *rippana*—a great... [use *na* when connecting with a noun]
桃 *momo*—peach
だ *da*—[copula; plain form of *desu*.]
さっそく *sassoku*—immediately; quickly; right away
切ってみよう *kitte miyou*—let's try cutting it
と *to*—[quotation marker]
包丁で *houchou de*—with a knife
桃 *momo*—peach
を *wo*—[direct object marker]

切(き)ってみました。

　すると、桃(もも)の中(なか)から元気(げんき)のいい赤(あか)ちゃんが「おぎゃあ」と出(で)てきました。

　おじいさんとおばあさんは、またまたびっくり。

切ってみました *kitte mimashita*—tried cutting (it)
すると *suruto*—upon doing so
桃の中 *momo no naka*—inside the peach
から *kara*—from (inside the peach)
元気のいい *genki no ii*—healthy; lively
赤ちゃん *akachan*—baby
が *ga*—[usually shows the subject]
おぎゃあ *ogyaa*—[sound of a baby crying]
と *to*—[particle for setting off quotations or sounds]
出てきました *dete kimashita*—came out
おじいさん *ojiisan*—old man; grandfather
と *to*—and
おばあさん *obaasan*—old woman; grandmother
は *wa*—[topic marker]
またまた *mata mata*—once again
びっくり *bikkuri*—surprised

子供(こども)がいなかったおじいさんとおばあさんは、その赤(あか)ちゃんを「桃太郎(ももたろう)」と名(な)づけて育(そだ)てることにしました。

子供 *kodomo*—children
が *ga*—[subject marker]
いなかった *inakatta*—didn't have (children)
おじいさん *ojiisan*—old man; grandfather
と *to*—and
おばあさん *obaasan*—old woman; grandmother
は *wa*—[topic marker; sets off the entire previous phrase as the topic of the sentence.]
その *sono*—that
赤ちゃん *akachan*—baby
を *wo*—[direct object marker]
桃太郎 *momotarou*—Momotaro, the Peach Boy
と *to*—[particle to set off a quote]
名づけて *nazukete*—named
育てる *sodateru*—to raise (a child)
ことにしました *koto ni shimashita*—decided on

おじいさんとおばあさんに大切(たいせつ)に育(そだ)てられた桃太郎(ももたろう)は、たいへん強(つよ)くたくましい若者(わかもの)になりました。

おじいさん *ojiisan*—old man; grandfather
と *to*—and
おばあさん *obaasan*—old woman; grandmother
に *ni*—by (the old couple) [used with the passive verb below]
大切に *taisetsu ni*—with great care
育てられた *sodaterareta*—was raised [the "*rareta*" is a passive construction that with "*ni*" shows Momotaro was raised *by* the old couple.]
桃太郎 *momotarou*—Momotaro
は *wa*—[topic marker]
たいへん *taihen*—very
強く *tsuyoku*—strong (and)
たくましい *takumashii*—burly; sturdy
若者 *wakamono*—youth; young man
になりました *ni narimashita*—became

そのころ、鬼(おに)がときどき村(むら)にやってきて、悪(わる)いことをたくさんするようになりました。

そこで、村(むら)の人(ひと)たちは、桃太郎(ももたろう)に頼(たの)みました。

そのころ *sono koro*—around that time
鬼 *oni*—ogre; devilish creature with horns on its head; bad guy in Japanese fairy tales
ときどき *tokidoki*—sometimes; at times
むら *mura*—village
に *ni*—to (the village)
やってきて *yatte kite*—came around; would come around
悪いこと *warui koto*—bad things; (do) bad things
を *wo*—[direct object marker]
たくさん *takusan*—many
する *suru*—to do (many bad things)
ようになりました *you ni narimashita*—began to do (like that)
そこで *soko de*—at that point; there
村の人たち *mura no hito tachi*—the people in the village [The "*tachi*" makes *hito* (person) plural (people).]
は *wa*—[direct object marker]
桃太郎に *momotarou ni*—to Momotaro
頼みました *tanomimashita*—pleaded; asked; requested

「桃太郎(ももたろう)さん、どうか悪(わる)い鬼(おに)を退治(たいじ)してください。」

「はい、わかりました。」

桃太郎(ももたろう)は、こころよく引き受(う)けて、鬼退治(おにたいじ)の旅(たび)に出(で)ることにしました。

桃太郎さん *momotarou san*—Mr. Momotaro
どうか *douka*—please; is there any way you could...; somehow...
悪い鬼 *warui oni*—bad oni; bad ogres
を *wo*—[direct object marker]
退治 *taiji*—get rid of; eliminate
してください *shite kudasai*—please do
はい *hai*—yes
わかりました *wakarimashita*—I understand; I'll comply
桃太郎は *momotarou wa*—as for Momotaro
こころよく *kokoroyoku*—willingly; gladly
引き受けて *hikiukete*—accepted; to undertake
鬼退治 *oni taiji*—getting rid of the oni
の *no*—[possessive marker]
旅 *tabi*—journey
に出ること *ni deru koto*—the act of going; leaving for
にしました *ni shimashita*—decided on

桃太郎(ももたろう)が旅(たび)にでるとき、おじいさんは、桃太郎(ももたろう)に刀(かたな)を渡(わた)しました。

おばあさんはきび団子(だんご)を渡(わた)しました。

「それでは、おじいさん、

桃太郎 *momotarou*—Momotaro
が *ga*—[subject marker]
旅に *tabi ni*—on a journey
でるとき *deru toki*—while leaving; when departing
おじいさんは *ojiisan wa*—as for the old man, he...
桃太郎に *momotarou ni*—to Momotaro
刀 *katana*—a sword
を *wo*—[direct object marker]
渡しました *watashimashita*—gave; handed to...
おばあさんは *obaasan wa*—as for the old woman, she...
きび団子 *kibi dango*—a millet dumpling
を *wo*—[direct object marker]
渡しました *watashimashita*—gave; handed to
それでは *sore dewa*—well then...
おじいさん *ojiisan*—grandfather

おばあさん、行ってきます。」

桃太郎は、元気に出かけていきました。

しばらく行くと、桃太郎は犬にあいました。

「桃太郎さん、そのきび団子を

おばあさん *obaasan*—grandmother
行ってきます *ittekimasu*—I'm leaving; I'm off
桃太郎は *momotarou wa*—As for Momotaro, he...
元気に *genki ni*—cheerfully; with courage; with strength
出かけていきました *dekakete ikimashita*—left; went out
しばらく *shibaraku*—after a while
行くと *iku to*—upon going; while going
桃太郎は *momotarou wa*—as for Momotaro, he...
犬 *inu*—a dog
にあいました *ni aimashita*—met; came upon
桃太郎さん *momotarou san*—Momotaro
その *sono*—that
きび団子 *kibi dango*—millet dumplings
を *wo*—[direct object marker]

ひとつください。」

「よし、私(わたし)と一緒に鬼退治(おにたいじ)に行(い)くなら、ひとつやろう。」

「はい、わかりました。一緒(いっしょ)に行(い)きましょう。」

ひとつ *hitotsu*—one (dumpling)
ください *kudasai*—please (give me)
よし *yoshi*—okay; well...
私と *watashi to*—me and...; with me
一緒に *issho ni*—with (me); together
鬼退治 *oni taiji*—get rid of oni
に行くなら *ni iku nara*—if you go...
ひとつ *hitotsu*—one
やろう *yarou*—(I'll) give...
はい *hai*—yes
わかりました *wakarimashita*—I understand; I comply
一緒に *issho ni*—together
行きましょう *ikimashou*—let's go; (I'll go with you)

犬は、鬼退治に一緒に行くことになりました。

もうしばらく行くと、今度は猿にあいました。

「桃太郎さん、そのきび団子をひとつください。」

犬は *inu wa*—as for the dog, he...
鬼退治に *oni taiji ni*—to go get rid of oni
一緒に *issho ni*—together
行くこと *iku koto*—the matter of going
になりました *ni narimashita*—became; decided (to go)
もう *mou*—once more; again
しばらく *shibaraku*—after a while
行くと *iku to*—going; while going
今度は *kondo wa*—as for this time
猿 *saru*—a monkey
にあいました *ni aimashita*—met; came upon
桃太郎さん *momotarou san*—Momotaro
その *sono*—that
きび団子 *kibi dango*—millet dumplings
を *wo*—[direct object marker]
ひとつ *hitotsu*—one (dumpling)
ください *kudasai*—please (give me)

「よし、私(わたし)と一緒(いっしょ)に鬼退治(おにたいじ)に行(い)くなら、ひとつやろう。」

「はい、わかりました。お供(とも)します。」

猿(さる)も一緒(いっしょ)に行(い)くことになりました。

よし *yoshi*—okay; well...
私と *watashi to*—me and...; with me
一緒に *issho ni*—with (me)
鬼退治 *oni taiji*—get rid of oni
に行くなら *ni iku nara*—if you go...
ひとつ *hitotsu*—one
やろう *yarou*—(I'll) give...
はい *hai*—yes
わかりました *wakarimashita*—I understand; I comply
お供します *otomo shimasu*—to go with; to join as a companion
猿 *saru*—a monkey
も *mo*—also
一緒に *issho ni*—together
行くこと *iku koto*—act of going; matter of going
になりました *ni narimashita*—became; was decided upon

またしばらく行(い)くと、今度(こんど)はきじにあいました。

「桃太郎(ももたろう)さん、そのきび団子(だんご)をひとつください。」

「よし、私(わたし)と一緒(いっしょ)に鬼退治(おにたいじ)に

また *mata*—once again; again
しばらく *shibaraku*—after a while
行くと *iku to*—while going
今度 *kondo*—this time
は *wa*—[topic marker]
きじ *kiji*—Japanese pheasant (bird)
にあいました *ni aimashita*—met; came upon
桃太郎さん *momotarou san*—Mr. Momotaro
その *sono*—that
きび団子 *kibi dango*—millet dumplings
を *wo*—[direct object marker]
ひとつ *hitotsu*—one
ください *kudasai*—please (give me)
よし *yoshi*—well; all right then; excellent
私と *watashi to*—with me
一緒に *issho ni*—together
鬼退治 *onItaIJI*—to get rid of oni

行(い)くなら、ひとつやろう。」

「はい、わかりました。私(わたし)もまいります。」

きじも一緒(いっしょ)に行(い)くことになりました。

行くなら *iku nara*—if (you) go
ひとつ *hitotsu*—one
やろう *yarou*—(I'll) give
はい *hai*—yes
わかりました *wakarimashita*—understand; I comply
私も *watashi mo*—me too; I also
まいります *mairimasu*—to go [more humbling way to say "*ikimasu*"]
きじも *kiji mo*—the Japanese pheasant also
一緒に *issho ni*—together
行く *iku*—to go
ことに *koto ni*—matter (of going); regarding (going)
なりました *narimashita*—became; decided upon

桃太郎(ももたろう)は、犬(いぬ)、猿(さる)、きじを従(したが)えて船(ふね)に乗(の)って鬼(おに)が島(しま)へ向(む)かいました。

鬼(おに)が島(しま)に着(つ)くと、鬼(おに)たちは城(しろ)の中(なか)で宴会(えんかい)をしていました。

桃太郎は *momotarou wa*—as for Momotaro, he...

犬 *inu*—dog

猿 *saru*—monkey

きじ *kiji*—Japanese pheasant

従えて *shitagaete*—to be accompanied by

船に *fune ni*—to a boat; in the boat

乗って *notte*—ride; get on

鬼が島へ *onigashima e*—toward Onigashima [the name of the island where the oni live]

向かいました *mukaimashita*—faced; headed toward

鬼が島に *onigashima ni*—on Onigashima Island

着くと *tsuku to*—upon reaching; upon landing

鬼たちは *oni tachi wa*—As for the oni, they...

城の中で *shiro no naka de*—inside the castle

宴会 *enkai*—party; banquet

していました *shiteimashita*—were doing (a party)

桃太郎と犬、猿、きじは、城の中に入り、鬼たちと戦い始めました。

犬は噛み付き、猿はひっかき、きじはくちばしでつつきます。

「いやー、これはかなわない。

桃太郎と *momotarou to*—Momotaro and
犬 *inu*—dog
猿 *saru*—monkey
きじ *kiji*—Japanese pheasant
城の中に *shiro no naka ni*—inside the castle
入り *hairi*—entered
鬼たちと *oni tachi to*—with the oni
戦い始めました *tatakai hajimemashita*—began to fight
犬は *inu wa*—as for the dog, he...
噛み付き *kami tsuki*—bit [literally, attach a bite]
猿は *saru wa*—as for the monkey, he...
ひっかき *hikkaki*—scratch; claw at
きじは *kiji wa*—as for the Japanese pheasant, he...
くちばしで *kuchibashi de*—with (his) beak
つつきます *tsutsukimasu*—to poke; to peck
いやー *iya*—[emphatic sound to show defeat and unpleasantness]
これは *kore wa*—as for this, it is...
かなわない *kanawanai*—unbearable; no match for (Momotaro)

親分、助けてください。」

鬼の子分たちは、親分を呼びました。

「うーん、どうした？おや、人間の小僧がやってきたな。」

親分 *oyabun*—boss
助けてください *tasukete kudasai*—please help (us)
鬼の子分たち *oni no kobun tachi*—the oni henchmen; oni followers [literally, oni children]
親分 *oyabun*—boss
を *wo*—[direct object marker]
呼びました *yobimashita*—called to
うーん *u-n*—yes?; hmm
どうした *doushita*—what's wrong?; what's this?
おや *oya*—oh?; my!
人間の *ningen no*—human
小僧 *kozou*—brat; youngster
やってきた *yattekita*—came
な *na*—[sentence ender to indicate emphasis or emotion; mostly used by males]

「私(わたし) は桃太郎(ももたろう)だ！鬼退治(おにたいじ)にやってきた。覚悟(かくご)しろ！」

桃太郎(ももたろう)は、おじいさんからもらった刀(かたな)で鬼(おに)の親分(おやぶん)を切(き)りつけて、とうとうやっつけてしまいました。

鬼(おに)たちは降参(こうさん)して、

私は *watashi wa*—as for me, I am...
桃太郎だ *momotarou da*—(I) am Momotaro
鬼退治に *oni taiji ni*—in order to rid of oni; to get rid of oni
やってきた *yattekita*—(I) have come
覚悟しろ *kakugo shiro*—prepare yourselves; be ready
桃太郎は *momotarou wa*—as for Momotaro, he...
おじいさんから *ojiisan kara*—from the old man
もらった *moratta*—received
刀で *katana de*—with the (received) sword
鬼の親分 *oni no oyabun*—the oni boss
きりつけて *kiritsukete*—slashed at; cut into
とうとう *toutou*—at last; finally
やっつけてしまいました *yattsukete shimaimashita*—won; beat; finished off
鬼たちは *oni tachi wa*—as for the oni; as for the ogres
降参して *kousan shite*—surrendered

「参(まい)りました。これからは村(むら)に行(い)って悪(わる)いことはしません。今(いま)まで盗(ぬす)んだ宝物(たからもの)をみんなあなたにお返(かえ)しします。」

桃太郎(ももたろう)は、たくさんの宝物(たからもの)を

参りました *mairimashita*—am defeated
これからは *korekara wa*—as for now on...
村に *mura ni*—to the village
行って *itte*—to go
悪いことは *warui koto wa*—as for bad things; as for bad conduct
しません *shimasen*—won't do (bad things)
今まで *ima made*—until now; up until now
盗んだ *nusunda*—stolen
宝物 *takaramono*—treasure
を *wo*—[direct object marker]
みんな *minna*—everything; all
あなたに *anata ni*—to you
お返しします *okaeshi shimasu*—return
桃太郎は *momotarou wa*—as for Momotaro, he...
たくさんの *takusan no*—many; much (treasure)
宝物を *takaramono wo*—treasure

持って、犬、猿、きじと一緒に村に帰りました。

おしまい。

持って *motte*—to carry
犬 *inu*—dog
猿 *saru*—monkey
きじ *kiji*—Japanese pheasant
と一緒に *to issho ni*—together with
村に *mura ni*—to the village
帰りました *kaerimashita*—went home; returned home
おしまい *oshimai*—the end

Momotaro Grammatical Notes

桃太郎 *momotarou* Just like "*ko*" in names usually indicates a woman's name, "*tarou*" indicates a male name.

1) むかし、むかしあるところに *mukashi, mukashi aru tokoro ni*

This is a very typical opening for Japanese fairy tales similar to "Once upon a time..."

2) おじいさんとおばあさん *ojiisan to obaasan*

Also common elements are an old couple: an old man and an old woman.

3) おじいさんは *ojiisan wa*

The "wa" topic particle is written with the hiragana は *ha*, but pronounced "*wa*." It is sometimes helpful to think of it as "as for...": "as for the old man, he..."

4) 山へたきぎを拾いに *yama e takigi wo hiroi ni*

"(to go) to the mount with the purpose of picking up fire wood." The "*ni*" makes "*hiroi*" (to pick up) the reason for going.

5) 川へ洗濯に *kawa e sentaku ni*

"(to go) to the river for the purpose of washing (clothes)." Again, the "*ni*" makes "*sentaku*" (to wash clothes) the reason for the old woman to leave.

6) 洗濯をしていると *sentaku wo shiteiru to*

"while doing the washing"—the "*to*" means "while" or "upon."

7) 大きな桃 *ooki na momo*

"a large peach"—Japanese adjectives are divided into two groups: -i adjectives and -na adjectives. *Ooki* can actually be either, but with -na adjectives, you attach a -na before nouns, as in this case.

8) どんぶらこ *donburako*

Japanese has a multitude of sound and action words. This one implies a splashing or plopping sound.

9) 大喜び *ooyorokobi*

"great joy"—adding 大 (pronounced *dai* or *oo* depending on what it is attached to) amplifies the noun, making it bigger or greater.

10) 大きな桃を見てびっくりしました *ookina momo wo mite bikkuri shimashita*

"Upon seeing the large peach, (they) were surprised"—the "*te*" form of "*mite*" explains the cause of why they were surprised. "Seeing, the large peach, they were surprised."

11) 子供がいなかったおじいさん *kodomo ga inakatta ojiisan*

"the old man who had no child"—This is a common construction: literally, "the without-child old man."

12) 桃太郎に頼みました *momotarou ni tanomimashita*

"(Village people) asked Momotaro"—the "*ni*" shows who was being asked.

13) ことにしました *koto ni shimashita*

"(Momotaro) decided (upon going)"—"*koto*" here means "thing" or "matter"; *ni suru* means "to decide upon."

14) きび団子 *kibidango*

Kibidango is a kind of dango or dumpling made with millet flour:

15) 行ってきます *itte kimasu*

This is a set phrase meaning, "I'm off!" or "See you later" and is often said when leaving the house.

16) 行くなら *ikunara*

"if (you) go"—行く *iku* (to go) + なら *nara* (if).

17) 鬼が島 *onigashima*

This is the name of the island the oni lived on. The "*ga*" here actually acts like the possessive marker の *no* as in, "the oni's island." You still see this form in place names in Japan.

18) 戦い始めました *tatakai hajimemashita*

"began to fight"—You can add the concept of "beginning to..." to just about any verb. Just form the -*masu* form, drop the -*masu*, and attach it to *hajimemasu*.

19) 親分 *oyabun* boss (parent) & 子分 *kobun* henchment (the children)

These two words tend to be used with bad guy organizations including the modern yakuza groups.

20) 覚悟しろ！ *kakugo shiro*

"be prepared (to be defeated)!"—This is often said before a fight in movies.

STORY ONE:
MOMOTARO, THE PEACH BOY
IN JAPANESE
桃太郎(ももたろう)

むかし、むかし、あるところにおじいさんとおばあさんが住(す)んでいました。

おじいさんは、山(やま)へたきぎを拾(ひろ)いに、おばあさんは、川(かわ)へ洗濯(せんたく)に出(で)かけました。

おばあさんが川(かわ)で洗濯(せんたく)をしていると、川上(かわかみ)のほうから、大(おお)きな桃(もも)が「どんぶらこ、どんぶらこ」と流(なが)れてきました。

おばあさんは、大喜(おおよろこ)びで、「こんなに大(おお)きな桃(もも)はみたことがない。うちに持(も)って帰(かえ)っておじいさんと一緒(いっしょ)に食(た)べましょう。」

おばあさんは、桃(もも)を家(いえ)に持(も)って帰(かえ)りました。

山(やま)から帰(かえ)ってきたおじいさんは、大(おお)きな桃(もも)を見(み)てびっくりしましたが、「これは立派(りっぱ)な桃(もも)だ。さっそく切(き)ってみよう。」と包丁(ほうちょう)で桃(もも)を切(き)ってみました。

すると、桃(もも)の中(なか)から元気(げんき)のいい赤(あか)ちゃんが「おぎゃあ」と出(で)てきました。

　おじいさんとおばあさんは、またまたびっくり。

　子供（こども）がいなかったおじいさんとおばあさんは、その赤（あか）ちゃんを「桃太郎（ももたろう）」と名（な）づけて育（そだ）てることにしました。

　おじいさんとおばあさんに大切（たいせつ）に育（そだ）てられた桃太郎（ももたろう）は、たいへん強（つよ）くたくましい若者（わかもの）になりました。

　そのころ、鬼（おに）がときどき村（むら）にやってきて、悪（わる）いことをたくさんするようになりました。

そこで、村の人たちは、桃太郎に頼みました。

「桃太郎さん、どうか悪い鬼を退治してください。」

「はい、わかりました。」

桃太郎は、こころよく引き受けて、鬼退治の旅に出ることにしました。

桃太郎が旅にでるとき、おじいさんは、桃太郎に刀を渡しました。

おばあさんはきび団子を渡しました。

「それでは、おじいさん、おばあさん、行ってきます。」

桃太郎(ももたろう)は、元気(げんき)に出(で)かけていきました。

しばらく行(い)くと、桃太郎(ももたろう)は犬(いぬ)にあいました。

「桃太郎(ももたろう)さん、そのきび団子(だんご)をひとつください。」

「よし、私(わたし)と一緒に鬼退治(おにたいじ)に行(い)くなら、ひとつやろう。」

「はい、わかりました。一緒(いっしょ)に行(い)きましょう。」

犬(いぬ)は、鬼退治(おにたいじ)に一緒(いっしょ)に行(い)くことになりました。

もうしばらく行くと、今度(こんど)は猿(さる)にあいました。

「桃太郎(ももたろう)さん、そのきび団子(だんご)を
ひとつください。」

「よし、私(わたし)と一緒(いっしょ)に鬼退治(おにたいじ)に
行(い)くなら、ひとつやろう。」

「はい、わかりました。お供(とも)しま
す。」

猿(さる)も一緒(いっしょ)に行(い)くことになりました。

またしばらく行(い)くと、今度(こんど)はきじ
にあいました。

「桃太郎(ももたろう)さん、そのきび団子(だんご)を
ひとつください。」

「よし、私(わたし)と一緒(いっしょ)に鬼退治(おにたいじ)に

行(い)くなら、ひとつやろう。」

「はい、わかりました。私(わたし)もまいります。」

きじも一緒(いっしょ)に行(い)くことになりました。

桃太郎(ももたろう)は、犬(いぬ)、猿(さる)、きじを従(したが)えて船(ふね)に乗(の)って鬼(おに)が島(しま)へ向(む)かいました。

鬼(おに)が島(しま)に着(つ)くと、鬼(おに)たちは城(しろ)の中(なか)で宴会(えんかい)をしていました。

桃太郎(ももたろう)と犬(いぬ)、猿(さる)、きじは、城(しろ)の中(なか)に入(はい)り、鬼(おに)たちと戦(たたか)い始(はじ)めました。

犬(いぬ)は噛(か)み付(つ)き、猿(さる)はひっかき、きじはくちばしでつつきます。

「いやー、これはかなわない。親分(おやぶん)、助(たす)けてください。」

鬼(おに)の子分(こぶん)たちは、親分(おやぶん)を呼(よ)びました。

「うーん、どうした？おや、人間(にんげん)の小僧(こぞう)がやってきたな。」

「私(わたし)は桃太郎(ももたろう)だ！鬼退治(おにたいじ)にやってきた。覚悟(かくご)しろ！」

桃太郎(ももたろう)は、おじいさんからもらった刀(かたな)で鬼(おに)の親分(おやぶん)を切(き)りつけて、とうとうやっつけてしまいました。

鬼(おに)たちは降参(こうさん)して、「参(まい)りました。これからは村(むら)に行(い)って悪(わる)いことはしません。今(いま)まで盗(ぬす)んだ宝物(たからもの)をみんなあなたにお返(かえ)しします。」

桃太郎(ももたろう)は、たくさんの宝物(たからもの)を持(も)って、犬(いぬ)、猿(さる)、きじと一緒(いっしょ)に村(むら)に帰(かえ)りました。

おしまい。

STORY ONE:
MOMOTARO, THE PEACH BOY
ENGLISH SUMMARY

Please try to tackle the Japanese first and use this only as needed.

Once upon a time, there was an old man and an old woman. The old man went to the mountain to gather firewood, and the old woman went to the river to do laundry.

While doing her washing, she saw—where the river flows—a large peach plopping and splashing toward her. With great joy, the old woman said, “I've never seen such a large peach. I'll take it home and eat it with the old man.” The old woman went home with the peach.

The old man, having returned from the mountain, was surprised to see the large peach. “What a great peach! Let's cut it right now,” he said, while cutting the peach with a knife. Upon doing so, from the midst of the peach came an energetic baby crying, “Ogyaa!”

The old man and old woman were once again surprised. The childless old couple decided to name the child “Momotaro” and raise him.

Momotaro, who had been carefully raised by the old couple, became a very strong and mighty young man.

About that time, oni had begun raiding the village and doing bad things. The people of the village asked Momotaro, “Momotaro, please get rid of the bad oni.”

“All right, I'll go.” Momotaro gladly accepted and decided to go get rid of the oni.

As Momotaro was leaving, the old man gave him a sword. The old woman gave him some millet dumplings (*kibi dango*).

“Well, then. Grandfather, Grandmother, I'm off!” Momotaro said and left with zeal.

After a while, Momotaro met a dog.

“Mr. Momotaro, please give me one of those millet dumplings.”

“Sure—If you go with me to get rid of the oni, I'll give you one.”

“Okay, I agree. Let's go!” And so the dog joined Momotaro to get rid of the oni.

After a little while, this time he met a monkey.

“Mr. Momotaro, please give me one of those millet dumplings.”

“Sure—If you go with me to get rid of the oni, I'll

give you one."

"Okay, I agree. I'll join you," the monkey said, also joining them.

Once again, time passed and this time he met a Japanese pheasant.

"Mr. Momotaro, please give me one of those millet dumplings."

"Sure—If you go with me to get rid of the oni, I'll give you one."

"Okay, I agree. I'll go with you," the pheasant said, also joining them.

Momotaro with the dog, monkey, and pheasant in tow, got in a boat and headed toward the Onigashima Island, where the oni lived.

Upon arriving at Onigashima, the oni were having a banquet in their castle. Momotaro and the dog, monkey, and pheasant entered the castle and began fighting the oni.

The dog bit, the monkey scratched, and the pheasant pecked with its beak.

"Uhh, they are too strong. Boss! Save us!" the oni all called to their boss.

"What? What's going on? Well now, did a puny human come here?"

"I am Momotaro! I have come to rid this place of oni. Prepare yourselves!"

Momotaro, with the sword the old man had given him, slashed at the oni boss, finally subduing him.

The oni surrendered, saying, "We give up. From now on, we won't go to the village to do bad things. The treasure we have stolen thus far, we give back to you."

Momotaro, carrying lots of treasure, left for the village together with the dog, monkey, and pheasant.

The End.

桃太郎さんの歌

Momotarou-san's Song

桃太郎さん、桃太郎さん
momotarou san, momotarou san
Momotarou, Momotarou

お腰につけたきびだんご
okoshi ni tsuketa kibidango
That kibidango (millet dumplings) on your hip,

一つ私に下さいな！
hitotsu watashi ni kudasai na!
won't you give me one!

あげましょう、あげましょう
agemashou, agemashou
I'll give you, I'll give you

今から鬼の征伐に
ima kara oni no seibatsu ni
From now, on to conquer the oni,

ついてくるならあげましょう
tsuite kuru nara agemashou
if you come with, I'll give it to you.

VOCABULARY NOTES:

桃太郎さん *momotarou san*—Momotarou (the Peach Boy)
お腰 *o koshi*—waist; hip
につけた *ni tsuketa*—stuck to; on; connected to
きびだんご *kibi dango*—A type of Dango (Japanese dumplings) made from the plant “*kibi*” which is millet.
一つ *hitotsu*—one
私に　*watashi ni*—to me
くださいな *kudasai na*—give (to me)
今から *ima kara*—from now
鬼 *oni*—oni; monster
の *no*—'s; possessive marker
征伐に *sei batsu ni*—to the conquest
ついてくるなら *tsuite kuru nara*—if come along

NOTE:
The first singer asks for Momotaro's millet dumplings. Momotaro answers, “If you come with me to attack the oni, I will give you the dango.”

Story Two:

The Tortoise and the Hare

with Running Gloss

うさぎと亀

あるところにうさぎと亀(かめ)がいました。

あるところに *aru tokoro ni*—in a certain place [a very common way to start a fairy tale in Japanese. Another clichéd opening line is むかしむかし a long time ago]

うさぎ *usagi*—rabbit

と *to*—and

亀 *kame*—turtle

が *ga*—[subject marker]

いました *imashita*—was; existed

うさぎは、亀(かめ)に言(い)いました。「亀(かめ)さん、あなたは世界(せかい)で一番(いちばん)のろいね。どうしてそんなにのろいんだい？」

亀(かめ)は、うさぎに答(こた)えました。

うさぎ *usagi*—rabbit
は wa— (topic particle) [Note this is the hiragana “*ha*” but when used as a particle as here, it is pronounced “*wa*.”]
と *to*—and
亀 *kame*—turtle
いました *imashita*—was; existed
に言いました *ni iimashita*—said to (the *ni* shows direction—in this case, the rabbit said ***to*** the turtle)
あなたは *anata wa*—(as for) you
世界で *sekai de*—in the world
一番 *ichi ban*—number one; the most [This is often used to mean “most”: 一番好き *ichiban suki* Liked the most]
のろい *noroi*—slow; dense [a bit more rude than *osoi* the common word for “slow”]
ね *ne*—aren’t you [*ne* is very versatile; watch for how it is used in different situations]
どうして *doushite*—why?
そんなに *sonnani*—to such an extent; that much
のろいん *noroiN*—The ん (short for *noroi no*) is used often to explain or ask for an explanation of things; somewhat casual
だい *dai?*—question ender, casual (use ですか instead)
に答えました *ni kotaemashita*—answered to (rabbit)

「なんてことをいうのですか？それなら、私(わたし)と競争(きょうそう)をしましょう。向(む)こうの小山(こやま)のふもとまで、どちらが先(さき)につくか、勝負(しょうぶ)しましょう。」

なんて *nante*—how…
こと *koto*—thing; matter
を *wo*—[direct object marker]
いう *iu*—to say
のですか？ *no desu ka?*—[this form of a question marker is used to show emphasis]
それなら *sorenara*—if that is the case…
私と *watashi to*—with me
競争 *kyousou*—race
しましょう *shimashou*—let's (race) [the ましょう form is an easy way to say "Let's..." For example, 食べましょう *tabemashou* let's eat; 遊びましょう *asobimashou* let's play.]
向こう *mukou*—over there
の *no*—(possessive marker)
小山 *koyama*—small mountain; hill
ふもと *fumoto*—base (of hill)
まで *made*—until; as far as (the hill); to (the hill)
どちら *dochira*—who
が *ga*—[subject marker]
先 *saki*—before; first
つく *tsuku*—arrive
勝負 *shoubu*—challenge; fight
しましょう *shimashou*—let's (challenge)

「よーし、やりましょう。」

うさぎと亀(かめ)は、競争(きょうそう)を始(はじ)めました。

うさぎは、亀(かめ)を追(お)い抜(ぬ)いて、どんどん走(はし)っていきました。

走(はし)りながら、うさぎは心(こころ)の中(なか)で

よーし *yo-shi*—Good! Okay!
やりましょう *yarimashou*—let's do it
うさぎ *usagi*—rabbit
と *to*—and
亀 *kame*—turtle
は *wa*—[topic marker]
競争 *kyousou*—race
を *wo*—[direct object marker]
始めました *hajimemashita*—started
追い抜いて *oinuite*—overtake [This is an example of two verbs stuck together to create a new meaning: 追う (follow; pursue) + 抜く (leave; omit; pull)]
どんどん *dondon*—rapidly; steadily
走っていきました *hashitte ikimashita*—ran
~ながら *nagara*—while (running)
走りながら *hashiri nagara*—while running
心の中で *kokoro no naka de*—in his heart; (he thought)

こう思(おも)いました。「どんなに亀(かめ)が急いでも、どうせ夜(よる)までかかるだろう。このへんでちょっと一休(ひとやす)みしておこう。」うさぎは、昼寝(ひるね)を始めました。

こう思いました *kou omoimashita*—thought like this [こう is used to mean "like this."]
どんなに...急いでも *donnani ... isoidemo*—however much ... hurries [どんなに…～でも is a useful construction. For example: どんなに上手に隠れても、見つけるよ。 *donnani jouzu ni kakuretemo, mitsukeru yo.* However good you are at hiding, I will find you.]
亀 *kame*—turtle
どうせ *douse*—after all; in the end; anyway
夜まで *yoru made*—until night
かかる *kakaru*—take (time)
だろう *darou*—think; suppose
このへん *kono hen*—this area
ちょっと一休み *chotto hito yasumi*—take a little break [notice the pronunciation is not "*ichi yasumi.*"]
しておこう *shite okou*—decide to do (take a nap)
うさぎ *usagi*—rabbit
は *wa*—[topic particle]
昼寝 *hirune*—nap
始めました *hajimemashita*—started

「ぐーぐーぐー。」

亀(かめ)は、その間(あいだ)にうさぎを追(お)い抜(ぬ)いてしまいました。うさぎが目(め)をさますと、亀(かめ)は、ゴールまであと少(すこ)しのところにいました。

ぐーぐーぐー *gu-gu-gu*—sound of someone sleeping
亀 *kame*—turtle
は *wa*—[topic particle]
その間 *sono aida*—during that time
追い抜いて *oinuite*—overtook
しまいました *shimaimashita*—ended up
うさぎ *usagi*—rabbit
が *ga*—[subject marker]
目をさます *me wo samasu*—wake up
と *to*—"and this happened"; A leads to B; "upon awakening, the rabbit..."
ゴール *go-ru*—finish line; goal
まで *made*—until
あと *ato*—after
少し *sukoshi*—little
ところ *tokoro*—place; position
あと少しのところ *ato sukoshi no tokoro*—just a little farther

「しまった。寝すぎた！」

うさぎがどんなに急いでも、亀には追い付けませんでした。

しまった *shimatta*—darn! I messed up!
寝すぎ *nesugi*—overslept [～すぎ is a useful ender meaning “too much.” A few examples: 食べすぎ *tabesugi*—eat too much; 言いすぎ *iisugi*—say too much; 勉強しすぎ *benkyou shisugi*—study too much (するー>しすぎ)]
うさぎ *usagi*—rabbit
が *ga*—[subject marker]
急いで *isoide*—hurried
どんなに急いでも *donnani isoidemo*—however much… hurries
亀には *kame ni wa*—as for the turtle
追いつけません *oitsukemasen*—couldn’t overtake
[追い付く *oitsuku* to overtake; 追い付ける *oitsu**ke**ru* **can** overtake; 追い付けません *oitsukemasen*—can’t overtake]

先(さき)にゴールした亀(かめ)は、うさぎに向(む)かってこう言(い)いました。

「うさぎさん、ずいぶん遅(おそ)いね。

先に *saki ni*—ahead of [here it means “ahead timewise.” The turtle passed the goal first. A very useful phrase is 先にどうぞ *saki ni douzo* Please go ahead (of me).]
ゴール *go-ru*—goal; finish line
先にゴールした亀 *saki ni go-ru shita kame*—the turtle that had already passed the finish line. [You can use similar constructions to add details about your subject. Think of such constructions as “The (subject) who (did this)”]
に向かって *ni mukatte*—faced; turned to face…
こう言いました *kou iimashita*—said this [the こう implies “like the following.”]
ずいぶん *zuibun*—pretty much; fairly [You can use this with anything needing a “pretty…” For example: ずいぶんあついですね。It’s pretty hot, isn’t it?]
遅い *osoi*—slow
ね *ne*—aren’t you?

さっきの自慢はどうしたの？」

うさぎは、なにも言い返せませんでした。

おしまい。

さっき *sakki*—past; just then (normally this is さき but can be pronounced さっき in speech.)
自慢 *jiman*—pride; boasting
さっきの自慢 *sakki no jiman*—the previous boasting
どうしたの？ *doushita no?*—what happened to… (the boasting)
[A more polite and very useful version would be どうしましたか？ *doushimashita ka?* What happened?]
なにも・・・ません *nanimo...masen*—not at all
言い返せません *iikaesemasen*—couldn't reply [This is another doubled verb: 言う *iu* (to say) + 返す *kaesu* (return)]
なにも言い返せませんでした *nani mo iikaesemasen deshita*—couldn't reply at all
おしまい *oshimai*—the end

Tortoise and the Hare Grammatical Notes

あるところにうさぎと亀(かめ)がいました。

In a certain place, there lived a rabbit and a turtle.

1) ## あるところに *aru tokoro ni*

In a certain place [a common way to start fairy tales; a way to not be specific about a location. ある人 *aru hito* a certain person; あるとき *aru toki* one time; ある本 *aru hon* a certain book]

2) ## うさぎと亀 *usagi to kame*

The Tortoise and the Hare [Note that the order is reversed from the English title: rabbit and turtle. Also, while the English uses more archaic terms “tortoise” and “hare,” the Japanese uses common and modern terms for the animals.]

3) ## が いました *ga imashita*

The turtle and the rabbit are living creatures, so you should use います instead of あります.

亀(かめ)さん、あなたは世界(せかい)で一番(いちばん)のろいね。

Mr. Turtle, you must be the world's slowest.

1) 一番 *ichi ban*

#1; the best [This is often used as a superlative ender: -est. For example, 一番おいしい *ichiban oishii* – the most delicious; with 世界で the rabbit is saying the turtle is the slowest *in the world*.]

2) のろい *noroi*

slow [*noroi* is not a nice word. It could mean "stupid" or "thickheaded" in addition to "slow." It would be best to not actually use this.]

3) ね *ne*

Aren't you? [The *ne* ender is very common in Japanese and can mean many things depending on context. Usually it is a question tag meaning "aren't you" or "isn't it?"]

どうしてそんなにのろいんだい？

Why are you so slow?

1) そんなに *sonnani*

To such an extent [*sonnani* and its cousins *konnani* and *annani* show a more than expected increase in whatever it is referring to.]

2) ん *n*

When the "n" is added to words, it adds emphasis or is used when explaining things.

3) だい *dai*

Question marker used to strengthen the force of the question.

なんてことをいうのですか？
What a thing to say!?

1) なんて *nante*

What (a thing to say) [*nante* is used to mean "what!" or "how!" to emphasize the ridiculousness of something said or done.]

私(わたし)と競争(きょうそう)をしましょう。
Let's have a race (with me).

1) しましょう *shimashou*

Let's do (a race) [*shimasu* means "to do"; the –*mashou* ender adds the "let's" meaning: 食べましょう *tabemashou* Let's eat; 行きましょう *ikimashou* Let's go.]

向(む)こうの小山(こやま)のふもとまで、
Until the base of that hill over there...

1) 向こうの *mukou no*

Over there [*mukou* means “opposite side” or “opposite direction,” but it is often used to mean a direction away from the speaker.]

2) 小山 *koyama*

Small mountain [adding *ko* to things makes it small: 子犬 *koinu* puppy; 小雨 *kosame* (irregular pronunciation) drizzle; light rain]

どんどん走(はし)っていきました。
(The rabbit) steadily ran on.

1) どんどん *dondon*

Rapidly; steadily; at a fast pace [Japanese has a number of adverbs like this that sound like the act itself. You can imagine the rabbit continuing to run past the turtle: *don don*.]

走(はし)りながら、うさぎは心(こころ)の中(なか)でこう思(おも)いました。
While running, the rabbit thought thus in his heart...

1) **走りながら** *hashiri nagara*

While running [Add ~*nagara* to mean "while ~" : 食べながら *tabenagara* while eating; 見ながら *minagara* while watching]

2) **心の中** *kokoro no naka*

Within his heart [like English, Japanese uses the heart as the seat of emotions and inner thought. In this case, it is what the rabbit is thinking.]

3) **こう思いました** *kou omoimashita*

Thought like this [Add *kou* to mean "like this": こう言いました *kou iimashita* said like this; こうやりました *kou yarimashita* did like this]

どんなに亀(かめ)が急いでも、
However fast the turtle may go...

1) **どんなに　～でも** *donnani ~demo*

However [Previously, we discussed *sonnani* to such an extent. This is the question version of that meaning. It is always used with the verb ender ても or でも. (sound changes depending on the word)]

どうせ、夜(よる)までかかるだろう。
After all, I'm sure it'll take him all night.

1) どうせ *douse*

After all; in the end; anyway [This is one of those adverbs that can really power up a sentence if used correctly. Listen for it and use it!]

2) 夜まで *yoru made*

Until night [~から *~kara* (from...) and ~まで *~made* (until) are very useful constructions: あしたから、あさってまで *ashita kara, asatte made* from tomorrow and until the day after tomorrow.]

3) だろう *darou*

I think [Use this to express a strong amount of certainty. The rabbit is pretty sure it will take the turtle all night.]

このへんでちょっと一休(ひとやす)みして おこう。

I'll just rest around here a little.

1) **このへん** *kono hen*

Around this area [The kanji for *hen* is 辺 and means "vicinity" or "area." *kono* means "this."]

2) **一休み** *hito yasumi*

A little rest [You'll probably recognize the kanji 一 meaning "one" and you may know that *hito.tsu* is a reading of that kanji. So, this means "one rest."]

うさぎが目(め)をさますと

Upon awaking, the rabbit...

1) **さますと** *samasu to*

Upon awakening [The と *to* adds the "upon..." meaning.]

亀(かめ)は、ゴールまであと少(すこ)しのところにいました。

As for the turtle, he was nearing the goal.

1) **あと少し** *ato sukoshi*

Just a little more [*ato* after + *sukoshi* a little]

2) ところ *tokoro*

Situation [*tokoro* usually a literal place, but as here, it can mean a situation or position.]

うさぎがどんなに急(いそ)いでも、

No matter how fast the rabbit hurried...

1) どんなに～でも *donnani ~ demo*

However (fast) [You should be familiar with this construction by now since it has appeared several times in this story.]

亀(かめ)には追(お)い付(つ)けませんでした。

(The rabbit) couldn't catch up with the turtle.

1) 追い付けませんでした

oitsukemasen deshita

Didn't overtake [*oitsuku* means to "overtake"; this uses the negative past –*masu* form: *masen* (negative) *deshita* (past)]

This is the same as 追い付くことができませんでした *oi tsuku koto ga dekimasen deshita* (wasn't able to overtake).

さっきの自慢(じまん)はどうしたの？
What happened to that boasting?

1) さっきの *sakki no*

The previous; a little while ago [Use の *no* to connect the concept of “previous” with “boasting”]
Use さっきの for something that just happened—not for something done yesterday.

2) どうしたの *doushita no*

What’s the matter; what’s wrong [What happened to the previous boasting? Was the boasting wrong?]

なにも言(い)い返(かえ)せませんでした。

1) なにも *nani mo*

Nothing [This always comes with a negative verb ending]

2) 言い返せ *ii kaese*

Retort; reply [言い *ii* speech + 返せ *kaese* to return]

Story Two:
The Tortoise and the Hare
in Japanese
うさぎと亀

あるところにうさぎと亀（かめ）がいました。うさぎは、亀（かめ）に言（い）いました。

「亀（かめ）さん、あなたは世界（せかい）で一番（いちばん）のろいね。どうしてそんなにのろいんだい？」

亀（かめ）は、うさぎに答（こた）えました。

「なんてことをいうのですか？それなら、私（わたし）と競争（きょうそう）をしましょう。向（む）こうの小山（こやま）のふもとまで、どちらが先（さき）につくか、勝負（しょうぶ）しましょう。」

「よーし、やりましょう。」

うさぎと亀(かめ)は、競争(きょうそう)を始(はじ)めました。

うさぎは、亀(かめ)を追(お)い抜(ぬ)いて、どんどん走(はし)っていきました。

走(はし)りながら、うさぎは心(こころ)の中(なか)でこう思(おも)いました。「どんなに亀(かめ)が急いでも、どうせ夜(よる)までかかるだろう。このへんでちょっと一休(ひとやす)みしておこう。」うさぎは、昼寝(ひるね)を始めました。「ぐーぐーぐー。」

亀(かめ)は、その間(あいだ)にうさぎを追(お)い抜(ぬ)いてしまいました。うさぎが目(め)をさますと、亀は、ゴールまであと少しのところにいました。

「しまった。寝すぎた！」

うさぎがどんなに急いでも、亀には追い付けませんでした。

先にゴールした亀は、うさぎに向かってこう言いました。

「うさぎさん、ずいぶん遅いね。さっきの自慢はどうしたの？」

うさぎは、なにも言い返せませんでした。

おしまい。

Story Two:

The Tortoise and the Hare

in English

うさぎと亀

In a certain place, there once was a rabbit and a turtle. The rabbit said to the turtle, "Turtle, you are the most slow-footed creature on earth. Why are you so slow?"

The turtle answered the rabbit, "Why would you say such a thing?! If that is what you think, then let's have a race. The first to get to the base of that small mountain wins."

"Okay, let's do it!"

The rabbit and the turtle started their race.

The rabbit passed the turtle and kept running.

While running, the rabbit thought within his heart, "However fast the turtle tries to go, it'll take until evening anyway. I think I'll just take a quick nap here."

The rabbit began his nap.

ZZZZZZ.

The turtle, meanwhile, overtook the rabbit.

As the rabbit awoke, the turtle was almost to the goal.

"Darn! I overslept!"

However quick the rabbit ran, he wasn't able to overtake the turtle.

Passing the finish line first, the turtle turned to the rabbit and said, "Mr. Rabbit, you're pretty slow, aren't you? What happened to all your boasting?"

The rabbit couldn't say a word in reply.

The end.

Kanji in Focus

Here are all the kanji that appear in *Usagi to Kame*.
Only the most common pronunciations are given and the most important are underlined.
The Hiragana after a ・represents the kana that is not included in the kanji
katakana = *on* readings; hiragana = *kun* readings

亀 turtle: かめ

言 speak; say: ゲン、ゴン、い・う、こと

世 period; world セ、セイ、よ

界 world; boundary カイ

一 one イチ、ひと・つ

番 order; watch バン

答 answer トウ、こた・え
私 I; me シ、わたし

競 compete キョウ、きそ・う

争 strife; contend ソウ、あらそ・う

小 small ショウ、コ、ちい・さい

山 mountain サン、やま

勝 win ショウ、かつ

負 lose; burden フ、ブ、お・う、ま・ける

始 start シ、はじ・める

追 chase ツイ、お・う

抜 pull out バツ、ぬ・く

走 run ソウ、はし・る

心 heart シン、こころ

中 center チュウ、なか

思 thought シ、おも・う

夜 night ヤ、よる

休 rest キュウ、やす・み

昼 noon チュウ、ひる

寝 sleep シン、ね・る

間 interval; space カン、ま、あいだ

目 eye モク、め

少 few ショウ、すく・ない、すこ・し

急 quick キュウ、いそ・ぐ

先 before; ahead セン、さき

向 face コウ、む・こう

遅 late チ、おく・れる、おそ・い

自 self ジ、シ

慢 arrogant マン

返 return ヘン、かえ・る

VOCABULARY

「」 quotation marks

A

赤ちゃん　*akachan*–baby
あなたに　*anata ni*–to you
あなたは　*anata wa*–(as for) you
あるところに　*aru tokoro ni*–in a certain place
あと少しのところ　*ato sukoshi no tokoro*–just a little farther
あと　*ato*–after

B

びっくりしました　*bikkuri shimashita*–was surprised
びっくり　*bikkuri*–surprised

C

ちょっと一休み　*chotto hito yasumi*–take a little break [notice the pronunciation is not "*ichi yasumi*."]

D

だ　*da*–[copula; plain form of desu.]
だい　*dai*?–question ender, casual (use ですか instead)
だろう　*darou*–think; suppose
出かけました　*dekakemashita*–left; went (to do washing)

出かけていきました　*dekakete ikimashita*–left; went out
でるとき　*deru toki*–while leaving; when departing
出てきました　*dete kimashita*–came out
どちら　*dochira*–who
どんぶらこ　*donburako*–plop; splash (sound)
どんどん　*dondon*–rapidly; steadily
どんなに急いでも　*donnani isoidemo*–however much… hurries
どうか　*douka*–please; is there any way you could...; somehow...
どうせ　*douse*–after all; in the end; anyway
どうしたの？　*doushita no?*–what happened to… [A more polite and very useful version would be どうしましたか？ *doushimashita ka*? What happened?]
どうした　*doushita*–what's wrong?; what's this?
どうして　*doushite*–why?

E

宴会　*enkai*–party; banquet
へ　*e*–to; toward

F

ふもと　*fumoto*–base (of hill)
船に　*fune ni*–to a boat; in the boat

G

が　*ga*—(subject marker)
が　*ga*—but
元気に　*genki ni*—cheerfully; with courage; with strength
元気のいい　*genki no ii*—healthy; lively
ゴール　*go-ru*—finish line; goal

ぐーぐーぐー *gu-gu-gu* - —sound of someone sleeping

H

入り *hairi*—entered
はい *hai*—yes
始めました *hajimemashita*—started
走りながら *hashiri nagara*—while running
走っていきました *hashitte* ikimashita—ran
引き受けて *hikiukete*—accepted; to undertake
ひっかき *hikkaki*—scratch; claw at
拾いに *hiroi ni*—to pick up
昼寝 *hirune*—nap
ひとつ *hitotsu*—one
包丁で *houchou de*—with a knife

I

一番 *ichi ban*–number one; the most
家に *ie ni*–to the house
言い返せません *iikaesemasen*–couldn't reply
行きましょう *ikimashou*–Let's go
行くこと *iku koto*–act of going; matter of going
行くなら *iku nara*–if (you) go
行くと *iku to*–while going
行く *iku*–to go
今まで *ima made*–until now; up until now
いました *imashita*–was; existed
いなかった *inakatta*–didn't have (children)
犬 *inu*–dog
急いで *isoide*–hurried
一緒に *issho ni*–together
行ってきます *ittekimasu*–I'm leaving; I'm off
行って *itte*–to go

いう　*iu*–to say
いやー　*iya*–[emphatic sound to show defeat and unpleasantness]

J

自慢　*jiman*–pride; boasting

K

帰りました　*kaerimashita*–went home; returned home
帰ってきた　*kaettekita*–returned (from the mountain)
かかる　*kakaru*–take (time)
覚悟しろ　*kakugo shiro*–prepare yourselves; be ready
亀には　*kame ni wa*–as for the turtle
亀　*kame*–turtle
噛み付き　kami tsuki–bit [literally, attach a bite]
かなわない　*kanawanai*–unbearable; no match for (Momotaro)
から　*kara*–from
刀で　*katana de*–with the (received) sword
刀　*katana*–a sword
川で　*kawa de*–at the river
川へ　*kawa e*–to the river; toward the river
川上　*kawakami*–upper area of a river; where the river flows from
きび団子　*kibi dango*–millet dumplings
きじも　*kiji mo*–the Japanese pheasant also
きじは　*kiji wa*–as for the Japanese pheasant, he...
きじ　*kiji*–Japanese pheasant (bird)
きりつけて　*kiritsukete*–slashed at; cut into
切ってみました　*kitte mimashita*–tried cutting (it)
切ってみよう　*kitte miyou*–let's try cutting it
子分たち　*kobun tachi*–henchmen; followers [literally, children]

子供 *kodomo*–children
心の中で *kokoro no naka de*–in his heart; (he thought)
こころよく *kokoroyoku*–willingly; gladly
今度は *kondo wa*–as for this time
今度 *kondo*–this time
こんなに *konnna ni*–such as this; like this
このへん *kono hen*–this area
これは *kore wa*–as for this, it is
これからは *korekara wa*–as for now on...
ことにしました *koto ni shimashita*–decided on
ことに *koto ni*–matter (of going); regarding (going)
こと *koto*–thing; matter
こう言いました *kou iimashita*–said this [the こう implies "like the following"]
こう思いました *kou omoimashita*–thought like this (こう is used to mean "like this")
降参して *kousan shite*–surrendered
小山 *koyama*–small mountain; hill
小僧 *kozou*–brat; youngster
くちばしで *kuchibashi de*–with (his) beak
ください *kudasai*–please (give me)
競争 *kyousou*–race

M

まで *made*—until
参りました *mairimashita*—am defeated
まいります *mairimasu*—to go
またまた *mata mata*—once again
また *mata*—once again; again
目をさます *me o samasu*—wake up
みんな *minna*—everything; all
みたことがない *mitakoto ga nai*—haven't seen; have never seen
見て *mite*—saw

も　*mo*—also
桃の中　*momo no naka*—inside the peach
桃　*momo*—peach
桃太郎に　*momotarou ni*—to Momotaro
桃太郎さん　*momotarou san*—Mr. Momotaro
桃太郎は　*momotarou wa*—as for Momotaro
桃太郎　*momotarou*—Momotaro
もらった　*moratta*—received
持って帰りました　*motte kaerimashita*—carry and return (home)
持って帰って　*motte kaette*—return holding (the peach)
持って　*motte*—to carry
もう　*mou*—once more; again
向かいました　*mukaimashita*—faced; headed toward
むかし、むかし　*mukashi mukashi*—a long time ago [This is the most common way to begin Japanese fairy tales.]
向こう　*mukou*—over there
村に　*mura ni*—in the village
村の人たち　*mura no hito tachi*—the people in the village [The "*tachi*" makes *hito* (person) plural (people).]
むら　*mura*—village

N

な　*na*–[sentence ender to indicate emphasis or emotion; mostly used by males]
~ながら　*nagara*–while (running)
流れてきました　*nagarete kimashita*–came washing down
なにも言い返せませんでした　*nani mo iikasemasen deshita*–couldn't reply at all
なにも・・・ません　*nanimo...masen*–not at all
なんて　*nante*–how…
なりました　*narimashita*–became; decided upon
名づけて　*nazukete*–named
ね　*ne*–aren't you?; isn't it?

寝すぎ　*nesugi*–overslept
にあいました　*ni aimashita*–met; came upon
に出ること　*ni deru koto*–the act of going; leaving for
に言いました　*ni iimashita*–said to (the ni shows direction–in this case, the rabbit said to the turtle)
に行くなら　*ni iku nara*–if you go...
に答えました　*ni kotaemashita*–answered to (rabbit)
に向かった　*ni mukatte*–faced; turn to face⋯
になりました　*ni narimashita*–became
にしました　*ni shimashita*–decided on
に　ni–by
人間の　*ningen no*–human
のですか？　*no desu ka*?–(this form of a question marker is used to show emphasis)
のほうから　*no hou kara*–from that direction
の　no–(possessive marker)
のろいん　*noroiN*–The ん is used often to explain or ask for an explanation of things; somewhat casual
のろい　*noroi*–slow; dense [a bit more rude than osoi the common word for "slow"]
乗って　*notte*–ride; get on
盗んだ　*nusunda*–stolen

O

おばあさんは　*obaasan wa*–as for the grandmother, she...
おばあさん　*obaasan*–old woman; grandmother
おぎゃあ　*ogyaa*–(sound of a baby crying)
追い抜いて　*oinuite*–overtake
追いつけません　*oitsukemasen*–couldn't overtake
おじいさんから　*ojiisan kara*–from the old man
おじいさんは　*ojiisan wa*–as for the old man, he...
おじいさん　*ojiisan*–an old man; grandfather
お返しします　*okaeshi shimasu*–return
鬼の親分　*oni no oyabun*–the oni boss

鬼の　*oni no*–the oni's
鬼たちと　*oni tachi to*–with the oni
鬼退治　*oni taiji*–get rid of oni
鬼が島に　*onigashima ni*–on Onigashima Island
鬼　*oni*–ogre; demon; bad guy in Japanese fairy tales
大きな　*ookina*- large; big
大喜びで　*ooyorokobi de*–with great joy
大喜び　*ooyorokobi*–great joy
おしまい　*oshimai*–the end
遅い　*osoi*–slow
お供します　*otomo shimasu*–to go with; to join as a companion
親分　*oyabun*–boss
おや　*oya*–oh?; my!

R

立派な　*rippana*–a great...

S

先にゴールした亀　*saki ni go-ru shita kame*–the turtle that had already passed the finish line.
先に　*saki ni*–ahead of
先　*saki*–before; first
さっきの自慢　*sakki no jiman*–the previous boasting
さっき　*sakki*–past; just then (normally this is さき but can be pronounced さっき in speech.)
猿　*saru*–monkey
さっそく　*sassoku*–immediately; quickly
世界で　*sekai de*–in the world
洗濯　*sentaku*–washing (clothes)
しばらく　*shibaraku*–after a while
しまいました　*shimaimashita*–ended up
しません　*shimasen*–won't do (bad things)

しましょう　*shimashou*–let's (challenge)
しまった　*shimatta*–darn! I messed up!
城の中で　*shiro no naka de*–inside the castle
城の中に　*shiro no naka ni*–inside the castle
従えて　*shitagaete*–to be accompanied by
してください　*shite kudasai*–please do
しておこう　*shite okou*–decide to do (take a nap)
していました　*shiteimashita*–were doing (a party)
していると　*shiteiru to*–upon doing...
勝負　*shoubu*–challenge; fight
育てられた　*sodaterareta*–was raised
育てる　*sodateru*–to raise (a child)
そこで　*soko de*–at that point; there
そんなに　*sonnani*–to such an extent; that much
その間　*sono aida*–during that time
そのころ　*sono koro*–around that time
その　*sono*–that
それでは　*sore dewa*–well then...
それなら　*sorenara*–if that is the case…
少し　*sukoshi*–little
住んでいました　*sunde imashita*–lived
する　*suru*–to do (many bad things)
すると　*suruto*–upon doing so

T

食べましょう　*tabemashou*–let's eat
旅に　*tabi ni*–on a journey
旅　*tabi*–journey
たいへん　*taihen*–very
退治　*taiji*–get rid of; eliminate
大切に　*taisetsu ni*–with great care
宝物　*takaramono*–treasure
たきぎ　*takigi*–firewood
たくましい　*takumashii*–burly; sturdy

たくさんの　*takusan* no–many; much (treasure)
たくさん　*takusan*–many
頼みました　*tanomimashita*–pleaded; asked; requested
助けてください　*tasukete kudasai*–please help (us)
戦い始めました　*tatakai hajimemashita*–began to fight
と一緒に　*to issho ni*–together with
と　*to*–[particle for setting off quotations or sounds]
と　*to*– "and this happened"; A leads to B; "upon awakening, the rabbit..."
と　*to*–and
ときどき　*tokidoki*–sometimes; at times
ところ　*tokoro*–place; position
とうとう　*toutou*–at last; finally
着くと　*tsuku* to–upon reaching; upon landing
つく　*tsuku*–arrive
つつきます　*tsutsukimasu*–to poke
強く　*tsuyoku*–strong (and)

U

うちに　*uchi ni*–to home; to the house
うーん　*u-n*–yes?; hmm
うさぎ　*usagi*–rabbit

W

は　*wa*– (topic particle) [Note this is the hiragana "ha" but when used as a particle as here, it is pronounced "wa."]
若者　*wakamono*–youth; young man
わかりました　*wakarimashita*–understand; I comply
悪いこと　*warui koto*–bad things; (do) bad things
悪い鬼　*warui oni*–bad oni; bad ogres
私も　*watashi mo*–me too; I also
私と　*watashi to*–me and...; with me

渡しました　*watashimashita*–gave; handed to
を　*wo*–[direct object marker]

Y

山　*yama*–mountain
やりましょう　*yarimashou*–let's do it
やろう　*yarou*–(I'll) give
やってきた　*yattekita*–came
やっつけてしまいました　*yattsukete shimaimashita*–won; beat; finished off
呼びました　*yobimashita*–called to
夜まで　*yoru made*–until night
よーし　*yo-shi*–Good! Okay!
よし　*yoshi*–well; all right then; excellent
ようになりました　*you ni narimashita*–began to do like that

Z

ずいぶん　*zuibun*–pretty much; fairly

More by Clay & Yumi

Ninja Penguin Talks Japanese in Japan
ISBN 978-1484825471
Price $12.99 USD

Hiragana, the Basics of Japanese
ISBN 978-1481863087
Price $8.99 USD

Kotowaza, Japanese Proverbs & Sayings
ISBN 978-1481904315
Price $8.99 USD

Japanese Reader Collection Vol 1
ISBN 978-1482373349
Price $8.99 USD

Japanese Reader Collection Vol 2
ISBN 978-1484191132
Price $8.99 USD

OTHER TITLES

Kanji 100: Learn the Most Useful Kanji in Japanese. ISBN 978-1482519815 Price $8.99
Japanese Grammar 100 in Plain English. ISBN 978-1482536621 Price $8.99

And: Katakana, Learn Japanese through Dialogues, Sound Words in Japanese, Haiku, Japanese Idioms, and others.

The Temporal
ISBN 978-1477406403
Price $12.99 USD

Fiction by CJ Martin

A Temporal Trust (Book two of The Temporal)
ISBN 978-1480119222 Price $12.99 [$2.99 eBook]

Two Tocks Before Midnight (An Agora Mystery)
eBook Price $.99

Tanaka and the Yakuza's Daughter
eBook Price $.99

DOWNLOAD LINK

Download Link for the MP3s:

http://TheJapanesePage.com/downloads/momotaro.zip

Thank you for purchasing and reading this book! To contact the authors, please email them at help@thejapanshop.com. See also the wide selection of materials for learning Japanese at www.TheJapanShop.com and the free site for learning Japanese www.thejapanesepage.com.

Made in the USA
San Bernardino, CA
04 April 2016